Musings
and
Memoirs

Edward McAuley

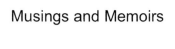

For my family and friends

Foreword

Every life is a story, and stories are meant to be shared. In these pages I've pulled together some of my writings and memories from across the years and I sincerely hope they will be an informative, heart-warming legacy for my family - as well as perhaps an interesting talking point for my friends, one that may bring a smile to their faces.

I've tried to include a variety of styles and materials. You may be surprised to find that over the years I even turned my hand to writing verse! I surprised myself, I must say. It started out as my way of dealing with my dear wife's Alzheimer's.

My relationship with Myrtle and how that disease affected us (all) is a big part of this story. My life was lived in two parts, one with Myrtle on a daily basis and the rest as normal as possible.

But there is a colourful mosaic of many other memories and reflections as well. There may be gaps in the telling, there may be overlap, there may be unexpected juxtapositions – but hopefully it all will prove interesting for the reader.

I have been described as a "tangential man". Friends and family know my tendency to go off at tangents in conversation and then have to ask, "Now, what was it we were talking about?" It seems my career, outlined in Part III, had something of a tangential nature as well, one thing often quickly leading to another, and I do believe I have held more jobs than would be the norm for people of my vintage.

May you enjoy perusing this collection of my "musings and memoirs," and may God be glorified in them.

Edward McAuley
June 2024

Contents

ISBN-9798326371348

Cover Photo by Jason Brodie

Edward McAuley

I

LIFE WITH MYRTLE

Reflections on my wife Myrtle, our marriage in 1958 and our introduction to Alzheimer's in her life in 1993.

Myrtle came home from a two-year stay in Canada and I fell in love with her at first sight in Albert Bridge Congregational Church. Of course, my selection was influenced by my dear mother who heard Myrtle at a ladies meeting in Malcolm Lane Mission Hall tell of her commitment to Christ.

I persuaded Myrtle to marry me in 1958 and not to go back to Canada until after I had finished my qualifications as a Chartered Accountant. I suggested we go together.

I organized the immigration papers in 1961 and was accepted but never got there because our house did not sell and Myrtle became pregnant with two children arriving in the one year.

In 1993 memory loss was evident in Myrtle, which was subsequently confirmed as Alzheimer's disease.

I sold my business in 1993, retired from that employment in May 2001 and took Myrtle to Muskoka Woods (a Christian camp in Canada managed by our son John) for four and a half months.

When Myrtle was told she had dementia (a word she disliked to hear in the following years) I knew my vow to her on our wedding day was to be tested. Thankfully God gave his grace to help.

If you have unexpected problems in your life that you were thrust into without any preparation or warning, you may find some solace in these words:

God is always a step ahead but yet close by.

I wrote *In Sickness and in Health*[1] at the commencement of Myrtle going into care.

Not an easy decision for Suzanne and me to make... We both cried as we saw her sad face at a little window in the ward door of Tardree House in Kells. My own health was not the best (I had had a heart attack and a stent inserted later in 2000) and Myrtle's consultant said she was also concerned about me as she could not obtain appropriate help from social services, even though she knew I would have endeavoured to be her carer.

Care was obtained at Bush Unit in Coleraine but after an incident where she pushed one of the residents she was returned to Tardree House for further assessment. Suzanne and I visited her there on a daily basis. She was moved to a ward in Holywell Hospital and ultimately to a residential facility, Cornfield Care Home in Limavady.

---

[1] P.14

The owners and staff looked after her (and me) so well that we refused to have Myrtle placed in a secure ward and she spent more than eight years being cared for there, till her call home to Heaven on 5 April 2013.

* * * * * * *

A Word of Encouragement on Dementia (Sept. 2004)

Has your dear one lost their verbal skills as their condition deteriorates?

Let me encourage you as you learn to live with this difficult situation.

Myrtle is my wife of 46 years (as I write) and is in a residential home. Over the last six months, besides losing her ability to walk, she has lost 95% of her ability to verbally express her thoughts and observations in any understandable way. Of course, I do not say to her that she is talking gobbledygook but rather convey the thought that as I am getting older I have a problem in hearing what she says and ask her to slow down a little.

Three instances over the last six months dissuade me from descending into complete despair. I cried because of my inability to help Myrtle who was uncomfortable and giving out a low and, for want of a better word, whinging sound. She stopped for a moment, seeing my tears and touched me saying "It will be alright."

The next difficulty was around St Valentine's Day. I found myself in the position again of not being able to bring comfort to Myrtle, still unable to understand one word of what she was saying, and I decided to go home, feeling it would be too stressful to stay and give her the evening meal.

I wheel her out of her room towards the dining room and she says perfectly "I love you."

The most recent occasion was when Myrtle was engaged in a three-hour session of loud shouting and making herself hoarse. No matter what I did or said it made no difference. I put my head in my hands and just prayed that she would find peace. To my utter amazement she interrupted her barrage of convoluted speech long enough to say "God bless him."

Thankfully there are many days without stress, but knowing that she has empathy with my position encourages me *inter alia* to visit daily and on a continuing basis tell that I love her very much.

* * * * * * *

For Richer, For Poorer

They've been going out together for over three years now

And their love has grown in the hours that away from work allow.

They cannot of each other see too much.

When they are together they steal many a gentle touch.

Arrangements have, with precision, been made

To confirm their love in marriage, for life, they said.

Vows before their loving Father they will repeat

Till death do part: and later then in glory they will meet.

For richer or poorer is one vow they do agree.

A tryst of love even if the path of life be poverty

Or, favourably perhaps by God's good grace, 'twill be prosperity.

They will accept either, and trust they do it thankfully.

Edward

In Sickness and in Health

God is in heaven lifted high
Yet by his Spirit draws close by,
Gives his comfort in our distress,
Assures he loves us more, not less.

The loved one who from us is parted
Is without that love abated,
For HIS arms their life surrounds.
To that love there are no bounds.

In the sickness of body and of mind
His grace and love are just so kind.
He will enable and empower
To trust him in each lonely hour.

Emotions, they express
Our humanity and our anxiousness.
But under and around each one
Whose faith is in the One above,
That knowledge of Eternal Love
Will keep us safely in The Faith
To help each other, through life till death.

And whilst at times we exercise concern
'tis for each one of us to learn;
God is aware of the tremor in each breast
And graciously smooths our brow to rest.
In this assurance and hope alive
That he will help us to survive.

Edward

Sure is it Worth it?

"She's just gone to lie on the bed,"
That's what the nurse has said.
The curtain is drawn, I suppose,
To hide her from view, and let her doze,
A prone figure stretched out full length,
Replacing what's been lost in escapades - some strength.
They say she walks (trots) a lot at speed.
Not surprising then, a rest is her immediate need.

I speak softly and call her name.
A response, for once, there is this time.
The arms shoot out and grab me tight.
"I was thinking about you all last night."
A smile a kiss, no not just one.
There are many more where that came from.

"So glad to see you and I love you so much."
The words they gladden my heart, I touch
And feel her face, it's steamy hot.
With cooling towel I bathe her face a lot.

To talk a while of friends and of things, is my intent.
A quiet smile, a face upon which is written - content;
And for her, a sleep, she quickly drops off.
The conversation was short, but for her enough.

Edward

What Puts a Smile on Your Face?

Kellogg's make a lot of breakfast cereals and one of their new offerings is Hunny B's. A recent advertisement endeavours to encourage children to eat their cereal but also suggest that parents might find the product satisfies mums' requirement that their offspring shouldn't miss breakfast any morning.

Surprising then, as a father of a 40-year-old daughter and a 39-year-old son, to find my wife, who suffers from Alzheimer's, holding tightly in her fist an extract from that advert. Prising it from her hand I discover that the motto says: "Put a smile on both your faces!"

A few tears and a Kleenex later I smile broadly. I read the message to her and she too smiles. You see, ten days earlier she had had a beautiful smile on her face, but now, having been moved to hospital, her expression has changed as she tries to adjust to the new surroundings.

She couldn't tell why she had torn it from the page. Short-term memory loss is one of the symptoms of this dreadful disease, yet presumably she has some subconscious awareness that smiles on both our faces is what is required at this present, very difficult time.

My thoughts run on to the joy that is in Heaven as angels rejoice when another soul receives the Saviour. Racing further, my thoughts are of my friends and family. Some may have forgotten or purposefully set aside the words they learned at home, in Sunday School or in church, about needing the Saviour. I pray that they may have their memories prompted by God and know the convicting and converting power of the Holy Spirit.

Now *there's* something to bring lots of smiles to lots of faces of lots of people AND angels – not just to two persons as suggested by the ad.

Edward McAuley
5th August 2003

* * * * * * *

Grace in Myrtle's life as seen by Edward

Some memories of evidence of grace in Myrtle's life that she lived assisted by our God and Saviour.

1. She never asked God or me WHY our first child was stillborn.

2. Her **forgiving** spirit when I tore the pocket out of a new Yves St Laurent suit which she had asked me not to wear when driving the church mini-bus.

3. **Graciously** receiving various people for dinner when I didn't tell her they were coming.

4. **Patience** when I arrive home from golf at 1am on a Sunday morning, having left home to play on Saturday morning at 10.30 – never doubting my explanation.

5. **Trustfulness**: she told our solicitor each time we moved house that she didn't want her name on the deeds because I would always look after her.

6. **Consideration** when I nearly put myself into bankruptcy by doing stupid things and she said, "I would have helped you, if only you had asked."

7. **Thoughtfulness**: when her friend Maureen died she told Vera, a mutual friend of Maureen's, "I know I can't be as close to you as you were with Maureen but if you would like, I could be your friend now." Of course, Vera is still here today.

8. **Concern** for the poor and needy, no matter their class, colour or creed.

Myrtle – A Tribute

A dark-haired, brown-eyed 21-year-old girl with an awesome smile is difficult to overlook. Especially true if your mother has already conveyed her praises to you in a very animated manner five days earlier.

The next high hurdle was having a future mother-in-law as her one and only son-in-law. I won her over using my natural charm, good looks and restrained arrogance. I put a restraining order on Myrtle not to go back to Canada until I had finished my accountancy qualification so that we could set up life together in Canada after that.

Continuing my romantic endeavours I persuaded Myrtle to join our badminton club and then encouraged her further to go on the regular weekly summer outings to Ballymacormick beach in Bangor and somehow or other got her to go back with me on the train to Belfast so that I could see her safely home.

In 1955, during her time in Canada, she became a Christian; I had become a Christian in 1954. Marriage intentions were discussed early on in our relationship when I was earning the colossal sum of £80 a year (*yes* - £80), and we got hitched on 15th October 1958.

Myrtle on top of the
Empire State Building
25.3.55

First night home after our short honeymoon I was told in no uncertain terms that study was the thing; so most evenings were spent with my head in the books. There was no way, she said, that she was going to be blamed for unsuccessful attempts at qualification.

In late 1959 we lost our firstborn as a stillborn son. Not once did Myrtle say, "Why me?" And that was a foundation stone of our marriage. We were God's children and he had promised to be our strength and power for each and every situation.

June 1961 brought the desired success of qualification and I set the practical steps in motion to fulfil the promise made about going to Canada.

Fortunately/or unfortunately, pregnancy put paid to that. Morning sickness on a bus from Castletown to Douglas in the Isle of man… evidential, that was.

Two for the costly price of one may be on offer! Two children in one year –Suzanne and John … in 1963 and 1964.

We learned a lot about the gift of Helps from Christian friends at that time as we struggled with two lively offspring! Our neighbour Mrs Crooks was a great help.

Christian teaching was part of our individual lives from childhood to teens, Myrtle in the Gospel Hall at the corner of her street, and me at Malcolm Lane Mission Hall in Belfast. Myrtle's parents belonged to Albert Bridge Congregational Church and she joined the Brownies there. During our courtship Myrtle recalled times I had pulled her Brownie hat off at the church parades. Would I ever?!

Myrtle expressed her faith by engaging in Christian service. She became the Irish Christian Endeavour Bookroom assistant, took junior members to Scotland for holidays, and her missionary interest increased as she met John and Anne Barnett in Scotland at that time. They worked in Brazil through Latin Link and now live there permanently.

Her care for others and interest in them became evident over the years and most of the time I wasn't aware that she had helped those who were in need either financially or by practical encouragement.

Myrtle did service in the RUC as a part-time constable, which she did until I started my own accountancy practice in 1978.

Myrtle was the teacher of our two children. I was a back-seat encourager. Principles instilled by example were learned at her knees and her introduction to a personal encounter with Jesus was a good foundation for their future. She was proud of their Christian achievements and I am happy to say that I endorse that wholeheartedly.

Our children give us great pride in who they are, what they do, and how they express their faith to all. Myrtle was a great helper in guiding them down their chosen career paths.

From 1989 when John was living in Canada we visited him every year. The day after I retired in 2001 we went to stay with John and Lori and see our two lovely grandchildren for four months.

John and Lori

Forgetfulness was what we thought Myrtle suffered from. But in 1993 at 59 years of age it became obvious that it was loss of memory, and in 1999 we were told that it was Alzheimer's. This is an extreme loss of memory leading ultimately in many cases to an inability to talk or walk; double incontinence; and being unable to feed oneself.

In the second year of my retirement we went to Canada for an intended three-month holiday, but if I can explain what happened like this – she fell off the edge... We came home after seven weeks, she was assessed and placed into care in Coleraine on 6th August 2002.

Her last eight-plus years were spent in Cornfield Farm Care Centre in Limavady. What can I say about Jervis and Jennifer Nutt and their committed staff of managers, nursing staff and carers?... Other than: You made us welcome and, I would venture to say, a big united family, where each of us wanted to give and make her so comfortable, especially when she couldn't walk or talk during the final six years of her special life. Thank you, thank you and many times thank you again!

Compassion was evident in all the staff, especially in the last few weeks as they helped her prepare to egress from this world to a higher and better place that final Friday morning. Thank you, thank you and many times thank you again!

From an accounting point of view, the 5th April is always a significant date – but from now on, for me, it will be doubly so.

Life will always be different for me, but I continue to live it in trust and in the same assurance as throughout the years since then: that Christ will keep his promise:

"Lo I am with you always."

Many of you have lifted us in prayer, encouraged and overwhelmed us by your kindness, and on behalf of Myrtle, Suzanne, John and myself, and Tim and Lori, another load of sincere and heartfelt thank-yous.

Suzanne and Tim

What a Difference a Postcard Makes

What's happening around me?
I hear and see but can't believe this is Reality.

I hear a voice that's raised to catch my attention
"A postcard, Myrtle, did I hear you mention?"
"Oh yes," she says, "I do declare
It's all the way from County Clare."
Some bright pictures on one side of the Cliffs of Moher I note
And on the other, words that someone wrote
In large hand for me to see
That the writer has remembered me.

There's something going on inside my mind...
There've been other cards of a similar kind.
One from Dublin showing Grafton Street
Where mussels are sold by Molly so sweet;
Another of painted doors of that fair city.
My, don't they look ever so pretty.
And what about the one of a box on a window sill
With flowers that overflow and still give me a thrill.

Many others have passed through the postman's hand,
He, quite unaware of the pleasures so grand

That each of them brings to me in solitary state
And brightens the room wherein I wait.

Edward McAuley

Here's another showing the GPO,
And one of Yeats in Drumcliffe, in Sli-----go.

Add to that a castle in Donegal
And one of sheep looking lonesome in all.

And on the reverse of one card that I read
This writer has reminded me once again
Of our eating some ice cream in Randals----town;
Trips to Lough Neagh, so recalls this writer
Made many a day for me so----- much brighter.

This writer can communicate in oral mode
In similar manner as with pen.
The memories, they please me once again,
Come quickly flooding into my humble abode.

He talks with knowledge of Coward and Anthony Quinn.
I suppose some will remember each one of them.
Stephen Boyd, the great Charlton Heston,
John Wayne and Lauren Bacall,
These are some that I---------- can recall.

I can't pull others from my confused mind,
But you will have episodes of a similar kind.

And those memoirs will come rushing in
As I recount my special times with him.

For the writer, the thoughts on these cards
Will in eternity reap rich rewards.
Like me, you'll be glad that you met my wee brother;

The likes of him, there is none other.
And each will in our hearts retain
Some memory that will help in times of real pain
And count it a privilege for us to have known
The scribe of these cards,
My brother Anderson----- John.[2]

Anderson family members visiting
Myrtle in hospital. Her brother John is in
the blue shirt.

---

[2] Myrtle's other brother was Bobby. Eddie read out this poem at John's funeral as an expression of her gratitude. She didn't attend the funeral and was unaware that both her brothers, John and Bobby, had passed away.

Thank You for Your Support on Our Journey

When Myrtle was placed into care after our Canada trip in 2002, we couldn't have known that this was the start of a hard journey that would last ten years, until she went to be with her Lord, 5th April 2013. She is now at peace.

Thanks To All

Some took the time to lift the phone
And others a pen to write
Some visited or made time to share a bite
To let us know that in all of this we aren't alone.

To each of you what can we say
But thank you for such love
And ask that you continue to
Remember us, before His throne above.

Day by day we know full well
That your prayers are not in vain,
As we face new and changing situations
And find grace to help again, again and again.

Never think that what you do is minimal
For in times of stress be sure
That what you've done or said or thought
Reminds us God is always faithful

Myrtle, Edward, Suzanne and John
May 2013

Edward McAuley

WS

Couple speak candidly about coping with dementia

Our love will last forever!

A local couple feature in an inspiring new publication by the Alzheimer's Society entitled 'Love is Forever'.

Launched in the run-up to Valentine's Day the booklet is a poignant reminder of the capacity people have to love and be loved as they face dementia together.

Edward and Myrtle from Coleraine recently celebrated 46 years of marriage.

Twelve years ago Myrtle's memory started to fail her. She was later diagnosed with Alzheimer's disease.

The couple remain very much in love despite the difficulties they have had to confront as a result of Myrtle's illness.

She now lives in a care home but is regularly visited by a devoted Edward.

He says: "It is always a pleasure to visit Myrtle and her smile makes the twenty-minute drive all worthwhile."

Theirs is a love that has seen many highs and lows, but despite dementia, it is a love that endures.

Neil Hunt, chief executive of the Alzheimer's Society says: "It is impossible not to be moved by the personal accounts given in 'Love is forever'.

"Each couple is an inspiration and gives hope to us all that love can survive despite the hurdles that are often placed in its way.

"Even though people in the late stages of dementia may seem to have little understanding of speech and may struggle to recognise those around them, this booklet shows their ability to respond to love and affection often remains throughout much of their illness."

HAPPY COUPLE...Edward and Myrtle from Coleraine who feature in 'Love is Forever.' CR7-141(s)

"Half of the people with dementia featured in 'Love is Forever' were under the age of 65 when they were diagnosed.

For a copy of 'Love is forever' as well as information about dementia please contact the Alzheimer's Society Northern Ireland office on 028 9066 4100.

4——THE COLERAINE TIMES, April 2, 2008

NEWS

Carer tells Council of dealing with dementia

The long goodbye

Una CULKIN

una.culkin@jpress.co.uk

A COLERAINE man took the brave step of telling his personal story at a Coleraine Borough Council meeting in a bid to highlight the daily stresses of living with dementia.

Ed McAuley told how he and his wife Myrtle were married in 1958 and set on out their married life with all the usual hopes, plans and dreams.

In 1993 his wife suffered a serious memory loss where she had absolutely no recollection of her own brother-in-law paying them a visit.

After a referral from her GP, Ed's wife was diagnosed with Alzheimer's at the City Hospital but no one actually told Ed until 1999 when it was just mentioned in passing to him by a doctor who assumed that he knew what his wife's condition was.

Her condition worsened in 2002 and Ed gave two examples of his wife's behaviour during a visit to their son in Canada.

"We were driving along and she tried to pull the steering wheel away from me and then she also tried to get out of the moving car," he said.

Ed described his wife's worsening condition as "dropping off the edge". She became morose and was no longer able to walk or talk.

"I now live two lives," Ed told the Council meeting. "I live each day with the uncertainty of what I will find each day I go to see her even though I know she is receiving superb care in Cornfield in Limavady.

"I once read a book which advised people caring for loved ones with dementia: your spouse is living in the moment, live in it with them and that is what I try to do now.

"My wife doesn't acknowledge me any more and sits with her head bowed most of the time. No one should have to go through Alzheimer's alone."

Ed told of the help and support he receives from the Causeway branch of the Alzheimer's Society and called for an assessment centre to be established in Coleraine rather than having patients, carers and consultants having to make the journey to Antrim.

NEED MORE HELP?

The Causeway branch of the Alzheimer's Society can be contacted on (028) 7035 8887

causeway@alzheimers.org.uk

Edward McAuley

THEN...Ed and Myrtle McAuley on their wedding day. CR14 184(s)

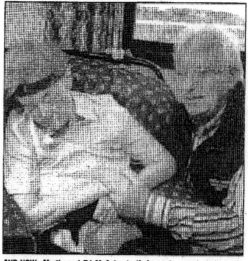

AND NOW...Myrtle and Ed McAuley in their most recent photograph together. Cr14 302(s)

SPECIAL TIMES FEATURE

Alzheimer's Society appeal to Coleraine Borough Council for support and assistance

COLERAINE Borough Council is to highlight the plight of those living with Alzheimer's and their carers at the highest level.

That was the unanimous message of support given by councillors to members of the Alzheimer's Society who gave a presentation at Tuesday's full Council meeting.

Adrian Friel, Causeway Outreach Worker, addressed the meeting along with a local man who is dealing with short term dementia and a local carer, both of whom gave personal accounts of what life is like dealing with Alzheimer's.

Mr Friel described Alzheimer's Disease as "like watching the person you love dying before your eyes".

Thelma Abernethy, Area Manager for the Society, said that 1,017 people were suffering from dementia in the Causeway area but added that the number is an under-estimation as many people are supported at home by their families and do not seek help.

There was unanimous support for a proposal made by Alderman David McClarty that Council write to the Health Minister making an appeal for extra resources for dementia care

and urging him to make treatment of the condition a priority.

Cllr David Barbour seconded the proposal and asked that the letter also be sent to the Northern Trust.

Cllr Billy Leonard asked that the letter also be sent to the Health Committee at Stormont.

Both these amendments were agreed by Alderman McClarty and the Council voted unanimously to support the proposal and the work of the Causeway branch of the Alzheimer's Society.

II

REFLECTIONS

A MISCELLANY

Christian Commitment

I attended the Christian Endeavour in Albert Bridge Congregational Church for many years.

At some point I made a decision to follow Christ and each month we, as active members, repeated the 'Active Members' Covenant', copy included below. I have endeavoured to fulfil the second paragraph, but fell short of that and subsequently rededicated myself to Christ in March 1954. It would be a good thing for each of us to do so, so why not make a covenant with God today?

Christian Endeavour - Active Member's Covenant

Relying on the Lord Jesus for salvation, and trusting in God for strength, I promise Him that I will strive to do whatever He would like to have me do.

I will pray to Him and read the Bible every day, I will support my own Church and its services in every way within my power, and throughout my whole life I will endeavour by His grace to lead a Christian life.

As an Active Member -

I promise to be true to my duties, to be present at, and take some part aside from singing, in every meeting, unless hindered by some reason which I can conscientiously give to my Lord and Master Jesus Christ.

If I am obliged to be absent from the monthly Consecration Meeting, I will, if possible, send an excuse for absence to the Society.

* * * * * * *

Edward McAuley

Some Favourite Moments

Over the years I have enjoyed a few favourite works by accomplished and recognisable poets and have included some of these. Charlie McMahon was my Cub-leader of the 35th Cub Scouts and he told a Rudyard
Kipling story about Mowgli - "Kill Shere Khan" (a tiger), serialised each Cub night just before we left for home.

He had a beautiful voice, I believe he was a lay reader in a Church of Ireland congregation in Newcastle, Co Down. He and John Arlott, a cricket commentator on the BBC, were favourite voices of mine.

IF
By Rudyard Kipling

If you can keep your head when all about you
Are losing theirs and blaming it on you,
If you can trust yourself when all men doubt you,
But make allowance for their doubting too;
If you can wait and not be tired by waiting,
Or being lied about, don't deal in lies,
Or being hated, don't give way to hating,
And yet don't look too good, nor talk too wise:

If you can dream—and not make dreams your master;
If you can think—and not make thoughts your aim;
If you can meet with Triumph and Disaster
And treat those two impostors just the same;
If you can bear to hear the truth you've spoken
Twisted by knaves to make a trap for fools,
Or watch the things you gave your life to, broken,
And stoop and build 'em up with worn-out tools:

If you can make one heap of all your winnings
And risk it on one turn of pitch-and-toss,
And lose, and start again at your beginnings
And never breathe a word about your loss;
If you can force your heart and nerve and sinew
To serve your turn long after they are gone,
And so hold on when there is nothing in you
Except the Will which says to them: 'Hold on!'

If you can talk with crowds and keep your virtue,
Or walk with Kings—nor lose the common touch,
If neither foes nor loving friends can hurt you,
If all men count with you, but none too much;
If you can fill the unforgiving minute
With sixty seconds' worth of distance run,
Yours is the Earth and everything that's in it,
And — which is more — you'll be a Man, my son!

The Thousandth Man
By Rudyard Kipling

One man in a thousand, Solomon says,
Will stick more close than a brother.
And it's worthwhile seeking him half your days
If you find him before the other.
Nine hundred and ninety-nine depend
On what the world sees in you,
But the Thousandth man will stand your friend
With the whole round world agin you.

'Tis neither promise nor prayer nor show
Will settle the finding for 'ee.
Nine hundred and ninety-nine of 'em go
By your looks, or your acts, or your glory.
But if he finds you and you find him.
The rest of the world don't matter;
For the Thousandth Man will sink or swim
With you in any water.

You can use his purse with no more talk
Than he uses yours for his spendings,
And laugh and meet in your daily walk
As though there had been no lendings.
Nine hundred and ninety-nine of 'em call
For silver and gold in their dealings;
But the Thousandth Man he's worth 'em all,
Because you can show him your feelings.

His wrong's your wrong, and his right's your right,
In season or out of season.
Stand up and back it in all men's sight —
With that for your only reason!
Nine hundred and ninety-nine can't bide
The shame or mocking or laughter,
But the Thousandth Man will stand by your side
To the gallows-foot — and after!

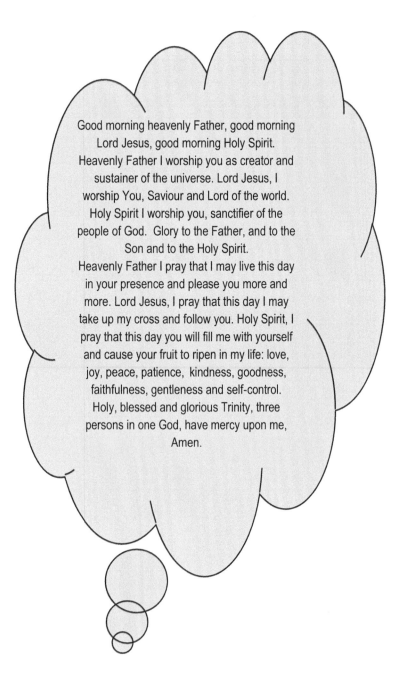

Good morning heavenly Father, good morning Lord Jesus, good morning Holy Spirit. Heavenly Father I worship you as creator and sustainer of the universe. Lord Jesus, I worship You, Saviour and Lord of the world. Holy Spirit I worship you, sanctifier of the people of God. Glory to the Father, and to the Son and to the Holy Spirit.
Heavenly Father I pray that I may live this day in your presence and please you more and more. Lord Jesus, I pray that this day I may take up my cross and follow you. Holy Spirit, I pray that this day you will fill me with yourself and cause your fruit to ripen in my life: love, joy, peace, patience, kindness, goodness, faithfulness, gentleness and self-control. Holy, blessed and glorious Trinity, three persons in one God, have mercy upon me, Amen.

Breaking Bread

In 2002 I came to live in Coleraine. I attend Mountsandel Christian Fellowship, a pretty decent lot of believers who have been supportive and stood with me, aiding in my service to Myrtle's needs.

We celebrate the breaking of bread and as some would say Communion and shortly after I commenced attending there, my good friend Arthur Williamson said to me that he was concerned that the folks attending may not truly appreciate how and why we celebrate the Communion. I went home that day and wrote the following verses - It's Not Like Winning the Championship.

I trust the reader will find some help in better understanding of the reasons for the Supper and how we conduct ourselves.

It's Not Like Winning the Championship

They sit around the table decked with colours of the team
Upon a spotless cloth there sparkles the victor's dream.
Reward for winning, a combination of fitness, feats and
planning.
The outcome of the struggle throughout months of committed
training.
There's food to eat and drink to sup,
Even a chance to touch the cup,
Some time to chat and talk
That creates a change in the way they walk –
Head held high and chest out swelling;
The stories of the passes, that flourish with the telling,
Reflective time for winners to compare
The victory with those of yesteryear:
And their conclusion, all are one,
That this was the best that had e'er been done.

In another place, some others on a Sunday morn
Sit around a table upon which are borne
Two symbols of remembrance there,
Not victor's spoils on which to stare.
No cup waiting to be caressed or kissed
Laid out there in simplicity transfixed;
No need for silver salver and elegant decanter,
Nor e'en expression of celebration or banter.

Each person will have the priority:
Taking time in self-examination.

Edward McAuley

Is there anything between me and God?
That needs correction or restoration?
And in similar vein between myself and him
With whom there is some confrontation.

It is a memorial observation by those who heed
The Lord's commandment to remember Him,
Whose sacrifice once offered is brought to mind
And His victory o'er the sin of all mankind.

Each guest at this moment may recall,
"It was my sin that caused His degradation,"
And spend some time in quiet contemplation.
The spread is not of gourmet fayre
Whose content and its presentation
Might win some culinary adulation:
It is the stuff of life, this bread and wine.

Take the bread and when 'tis broken
Give thanks to God for the body, of this a token
Of His dear Son whose torso bore
More wounds, more marred than any man before.

The table bears the wine, a symbol of His blood,
Poured out a willing sacrifice in transforming
Man, to be sons of God.
They take that wine and as instructed

Offer thanks to God in heaven
For the sacrifice of His dear Son

Who now sits on His right above,
Victory o'er sin and death now won.

The memorial recalls the agony of the cross
As we break the bread and pour the cup.
And yet for all partaking there is a recognition
This proclamation comes with limitation;
For the timescale is restricted, *Till He Come*.
And we, with all those who love His appearing
Will, in His Father's kingdom, drink with Him.

None may follow to this Heaven
Unless their sins on earth are forgiven.
Life is in the blood, the Scriptures do declare,
And yet by Christ's death we all eternal life may share.
But without faith in the precious blood once shed,
No cleansing can take place
Requiring man's repentance,
God's mercy and his grace.

Edward McAuley
March 1st 2003

THOUGHTS ON THE BREAKING OF BREAD

A man ought to examine himself	SELF-EXAMINATION
When you come together	A CONVOCATION
...each of you goes ahead without waiting for anybody else	NO DISCRIMINATION
Whenever you eat this bread and drink this cup you proclaim the Lord's death	PROCLAMATION
...until	WITH LIMITATION
He comes	IN ANTICIPATION

Living for Eternal Glory

In 1954 I committed my life to Christ and endeavoured by his grace to live a disciplined life. Unfortunately, I confess, I have failed Him and some of my colleagues and friends, which I regret, but the Scriptures say:

"If we confess our sin, He is able to forgive us our sin and cleanse us from all unrighteousness."

The following passage from Scripture reminds us that as Christians we are expected to do the good works that God has provided for us to do and will be rewarded, but the rewards are for faithful service, not for our salvation, which is only available through accepting the offering of the one and only sacrifice for sin forever, viz the finished work of Christ on the Cross, which gives us assurance of salvation.

Nice Surprises on the Last Day (Matthew 25: 21 - 40)

*When the Son of Man comes in his glory, and all the angels
with him, then he will sit on his glorious throne. Before him will
be gathered all the nations, and he will separate people one
from another as a shepherd separates the sheep from the
goats. And he will place the sheep on his right,
but the goats on the left.*

*Then the King will say to those on his right, 'Come, you who are
blessed by my Father, inherit the kingdom prepared for you
from the foundation of the world. For I was hungry and you
gave me food, I was thirsty and you gave me drink, I was a
stranger and you welcomed me, I was naked and you clothed
me, I was sick and you visited me, I was in prison
and you came to me.'*

*Then the righteous will answer him, saying, 'Lord, when did we
see you hungry and feed you, or thirsty and give you drink? And
when did we see you a stranger and welcome you, or naked
and clothe you? And when did we see you sick or in prison and
visit you?' And the King will answer them, 'Truly, I say to you, as
you did it to one of the least of these my brothers,
you did it to me.'*

(ESV)

Christianity Lived Out

In 2007 I received correspondence from Margaret and Jimmy Tiggerdene in Glasgow. They were celebrating 50 years of married life and wanted to come back to Castle Erin, Portrush, the place where they had spent their honeymoon, as had Myrtle and I. It was now closed down however, so I invited them to stay at my home. It was a great time with them and we still correspond.

Afterwards, Jimmy and Margaret sent me this poem: "*I'd Rather See a Sermon.*"

I'd Rather See A Sermon
By Edgar A. Guest (1881 - 1959)

I'd rather see a sermon than hear one any day;
I'd rather one should walk with me than merely tell the way.
The eye's a better pupil and more willing than the ear,
Fine counsel is confusing, but example's always clear;
And the best of all the preachers are the men who live their
creeds,
For to see good put in action is what everybody needs.

I soon can learn to do it if you'll let me see it done;
I can watch your hands in action, but your tongue too fast may
run.
And the lecture you deliver may be very wise and true,
But I'd rather get my lessons by observing what you do;
For I might misunderstand you and the high advice you give,
But there's no misunderstanding how you act and how you live.

When I see a deed of kindness, I am eager to be kind.
When a weaker brother stumbles and a strong man stays behind
Just to see if he can help him, then the wish grows strong in me
To become as big and thoughtful as I know that friend to be.
And all travellers can witness that the best of guides today
Is not the one who tells them, but the one who shows the way.

One good man teaches many, men believe what they behold;
One deed of kindness noticed is worth forty that are told.
Who stands with men of honor learns to hold his honor dear,
For right living speaks a language which to everyone is clear.
Though an able speaker charms me with his eloquence, I say,
I'd rather see a sermon than hear one, any day.

Public Domain

Jimmy and Margaret Tiggerdene

Always Be Presentable

Commencing work at the age of 15 in Broadway Damask as a factory wages clerk and then as an audit clerk in James Baird and Co, I soon realised that dressing properly was the order of the day. For most of my working life a tailor's shop at the Hollywood Arches in Belfast had provided me with good suits and ties. The shop was owned by Mr Cochrane, the father of a dear friend of recent years, Colin.

In later years my shirts come from Charles Tyrwhitt in London, less than 20 now 40 Quid a throw; instead of £69 a time. Its founder is Nicholas Wheeler and he would frequently write a letter of appeal if the volume of online shopping was dwindling. On one occasion I replied in rhyming verse with *Ode to Wheeler*.

Wonderful what comes into your head when you are challenged to purchase another Tyrwhitt shirt, tie trousers and even cufflinks and socks!

I haven't watched *Dress to Impress* on TV, but have tried my best - and Myrtle's intervention, always to be presentable (as you never knew who you would meet) still guides me to this day.

Ode to Wheeler

His greatest wish for all his customers
Is to see each dressed with shirts in classic styles
And when no purchase order comes his way
His chin doth drop in unbelieved dismay.

"Why, oh why, can't they have some sense
And purchase now and save some pence?
Two shirts for the price of one
Surely they're not all by nature simpletons.
No advantage at this moment have they taken,
Have they all their minds forsaken?!
How shall I move this stock so rare
And make room more in that store, though there's space to spare?"
"I know, I know," he doth exclaim.
"Open an outlet ne'er seen on planet Earth
At a place where of many shirts there is a dearth."

He settled here and rushes there; all is ready, 'twill be soon
To that outlet in a crater on the dark side of the moon:
"That's where my customers have gone," is what he thinks
And packs his bags with ties and shirts and some cufflinks.

I'm glad to say I don't live there in lunar sand.
I'm taking up his offer here from this green land
By ordering a shirt that's made to size
With another added free, what a surprise.

So keep sending to my address that's down below
And make delivery quick, not slow.
And upon Nicholas's return from outer space
May this order have brought a smile to his face.

Edward McAuley

173

Dear Mr McAuley

Keep them coming. I attached a little gift.
Call it a thank you for the laughs.

You deserve it.

Nick Wheeler.

Founder

20%off

Mr Edward McAuley

CUSTOMER NUMBER: 8319248
OFFER CODE: JZDQG29E7F3W

CHARLES TYRWHITT

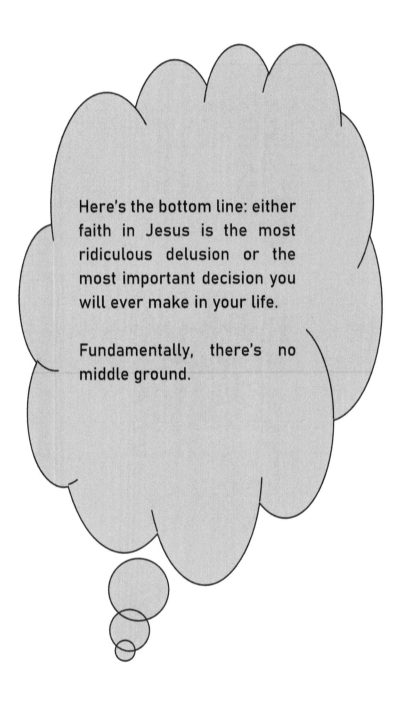

Here's the bottom line: either faith in Jesus is the most ridiculous delusion or the most important decision you will ever make in your life.

Fundamentally, there's no middle ground.

Love, Love, Love....

When I commenced self-employment in January 1978 my office was the dining room in our home in Crawford Park, Belfast, and during that year and a half I listened to Radio Ulster, enjoying the craic supplied by George Jones and Sadie.

One song, "Hugs and Butterfly Kisses", was requested and was for a daughter preparing for her wedding. That was overlooked by George and I penned these lines. The truth expressed is just as applicable today.

Hugs and Butterfly Kisses

I listened to the George Jones show the other day
Enjoyed the different kinds of songs that were played.
Some chosen, no doubt, by George or Sadie in 60s or 70s style,
But one, upon request, brought a tear to my eye.

A special request for a daughter on her wedding day.
Because of other pressures the record was not played.
No doubt the friends whose choice it was, were disappointed too?
But George made things alright, as he is wont to do.

Hugs and *butterfly kisses* were given each morning and at night,
Because one little girl thought she must've done something right.
But I wondered if the songwriter considered the parents' point of view
'Cos these expressions were no reward for things well done – 'tis true.

Parents do from time to time encourage with a carrot or a stick,
But to express their love, no need to resort to such a lowly trick.
No matter what the children do, we still love them, oh so much,
And when they're bad or good they still should have our touch.

Sometimes we have to correct them and administer discipline,
But that might help them think of others and take it on the chin.
Don't please only reward the kids when they are so good.
Try to see the best in them when heads do seem like wood –
Not listening, nor taking in one word of what we say:
But better they remember LOVE, upon their wedding day.

Edward McAuley
ca. 1980.

On Submission

My son was reading a book written by Dr Helen Roseveare called Living Fellowship. She was writing about the believer's relationship with God.

In the book you read of "God as the hub of our wheel and we are the spokes reaching out to the rim of the world."

When you and I experience this true fellowship with God we will know because it will involve submission, service, suffering and the submitting of our will to God.

Someone wrote the following words some time ago.

Not ours to know the reason why
Unanswered is our prayer,
But ours to wait for God's own time
To lift the cross we bear.

Not ours to know the reason why
From loved ones we must part,
But ours to live in faith and hope
Though bleeding be the heart.

Not ours to know the reason why
This anguish, strife and pain,
But ours to know a crown of thorns,
Thy grace for us to gain.

A cross, a bleeding heart, a crown,
What greater gifts are given?
Be still, my heart, and murmur not,
These are the keys to heaven.

'Tis ours to know the better part
Whereby a crown is won,
Then loving God I ask not why,
"Thy will, not mine, be done."

Yea, Thy way, Lord, not mine, I pray,
I give to Thee my will,
And humbly seek Thy grace and aid,
This better part to fill.

It was not always thus with me,
I loved my way the best,
But that is past, Thy way is mine,
In it alone is rest.

Anon

Missionary Interest

Transcript of a short talk I gave in Mountsandel Christian Fellowship in 2023.

My first introduction to giving towards missionary work was at probably at nine years of age.

Here is a half-penny coin...

Any elderly person recall that?!

It ran from 1945 till 1969 and was phased out in preparation for decimalisation.

What value was it.....(a question for *golden oldies* !)

- It was worth 1 / 480th of a £1.

Can anybody describe it?

- One side had the King's head....The other: a picture of a beautiful, many-sailed yacht.

The main church I attended supported the Congregational Mission, The London Missionary Society. One part of the mission's work was in the Gilbert and Ellice islands in the Pacific.

They raised interest and support from children by collection of those copper coins called *ha'pennies* to purchase a ship named *The John Williams*.

I supported the efforts and became 100% committed to sharing the work of the LMS until the Society drifted into association with an organisation which was not in keeping with what most believed.

I supported other societies across the years. One I had heard of but didn't support at the time was <u>Open Doors</u>.

A few weeks ago I picked up a pamphlet at the Portstewart Keswick Convention and read about its foundation by Brother Andrew in 1955, aged 27.

The first smuggled Bibles were to Poland

Brother Andrew went on to smuggle millions of Bibles and New Testaments into countries where Christians were persecuted, even murdered. The statistics are amazing. In 1981 one million Bibles were delivered to China in just one night (Operation Pearl). In 1989 a million New Testaments were smuggled into Russia.

Brother Andrew died in 2022. But the work continues today.

The crux of my talk this morning is to say we have in our own congregation, a lady, Rachel Coural, who represents the international branch of Open Doors.

I was challenged by what I read in that leaflet and now I'd like to challenge you.

Are you interested in reading a best-seller book that has sold millions of copies and still does? If so, I am offering the first ten people a free gift of Brother Andrew's book *God's Smuggler* which was updated in 2017.

The gift has a BUT...

If you take one there is no cost to you. But it is governed by one condition: after you have read it, each recipient will pass it on to someone else.

Any takers? I have three copies with me and will get another seven if you give me your contact number or address at the end of the service.

You can also speak to Rachel at any time She is here and has an office upstairs in this building. I am sure she would be pleased to deal with questions and would welcome any support.

I am reading *God's Smuggler* at present

May each find it as challenging as I do!

Thank you.

III

THE TANGENTIAL MAN

The McAuley family in 1953

A Look Back Over the Years

Today as I write these particular lines (15th Oct. 2019) I reflect that it would have been our 61st wedding anniversary and my thoughts lead me to think of how God helped us across the years, and still does help me today.

This prompts me to reflect that it might be good to consider various aspects of my Christian life commencing 26th March 1954.

Albert Bridge Congregational Church was where God convicted me of my sin as a sinner and my need of salvation only to be found in the work of Christ on the cross.

> Oh what a Saviour that He should die for me
> From condemnation he hath set me free
> For who so ever believes on Him
> Hath everlasting life.

The Bible tells me that the Holy Spirit is the third part of The Trinity (Father, Son and Holy Spirit); that the Holy Spirit convicts of sin, righteousness and judgement and regenerates the soul who confesses their sin and accepts that redemption has been purchased by the shed blood of Christ on the Cross.

It would be wrong of me to give the impression that 1954 was the first time that God convicted me of sin in my life.

Paul writes to Timothy as follows:

> "From a child thou hast known the holy scriptures which are able to make you wise unto salvation."

I was born to Henry and Agnes Elizabeth McAuley, together with my twin sister in 25 Victor Street on 1st March 1936. We were the final addition to the line of children. There were five other boys: Henry, Jim, David J, Carlisle and William Thomas.[3]

---

[3] See photo on p.63

Eddie and Sister
Margaret at 4

The Malcolm Lane Mission Hall was a big part of my life from age two to fourteen (and subsequently again when I joined the Oversight after my conversion at age 18).

I recall the teachers there who introduced me to the Truth about myself "being born in sin and shaped in iniquity." I attended morning and afternoon Sunday Schools where several men and one woman taught me the things a child should know. There was Mark Walker, his brother-in-law Marshall Caughey, Mrs Martha Deas, Arthur McCune and Mr RD McCaw, the joint founder of the Mission Hall. His co-founder, Mr Spence died whilst preaching in the Hall and to my memory, my mother came to know salvation in the Lord at that service.

Malcolm Lane Mission Hall was a place of worship and Christian teaching from 1895 to 1975. The building was later destroyed in a fire.

Church memorial window for Eddie's mother, Agnes Elizabeth

My dad encouraged my next older brother to take me with him to the 35th Cub Group in Albert Bridge Congregational Church halls, even though I was too young to join. Of course, I did anyway and that is not surprising as I was the youngest of six male children. Carl didn't join the Scouts but became a founding member of the 56th Boys Brigade.

All my siblings were known by so many people that I, as the youngest, had a really difficult time living up to their lives. I recall vividly when I was messing around in the class line at lunchtime in Park Parade School and was instructed by the teacher, "McAuley go and wait for me in room 12. "As the members of that class filed past they said "Mr Cuddy will bounce you of the wall" etc. Of course, when Mr Cuddy came to the class all he could say was, "What about Harry, Jim, David, Carl, William. How are they getting on? Go on to your class and don't mess up anymore." ...Phew!

Charlie McMahon was the Cubmaster. I loved to hear him tell the Rudyard Kipling's Jungle Book stories featuring Mowgli. *Kill Shere Khan*, Kill *Shere Khan* (the tiger) we would chant, as we demonstrated plunging the dagger into the back of the animal each time the *Kill* word was used.

He had a wonderful voice; he was a lay-reader in one of the Church of Ireland congregations and I could imagine him at the rostrum reading the Scriptures. Mr McMahon, I discovered a good few years later, was an accountant at Stevenson and Turner.

When I was 12 my friend David Moffett and I joined another Scout Group, the *37th Belfast*. My brother William, who is four years older than me was a member there. It was brilliant troop and they had their own Scout Hall in Lisbon Street, just off the Albertbridge Road. This meant the hall was not controlled by any church and so lots of things happened there that would not normally have the approval of a church.

Stanley Gibson was the Scout master and Harold Johnston the group Scout master. Harold was the manager of a Co-op Store on the Ormeau Road at Rosetta and lived in Ardenlee Avenue. Stanley had a corner grocery store at Rathmore/Shamrock streets. Stanley could never remember the name of each Scout and he would just call them John. He had fantastic blue eyes and these were always darting about taking in all that was going on and correcting those who needed disciplining.

I enjoyed calling into his shop on the way home from Park Parade School practically every day until I passed the Qualifying Exam and left to attend Belfast Inst, (RBAI), where I stayed for three years from 1948 till 1951. I passed the Junior Certificate exam with reasonable success and joined Broadway Damask Company as factory wages clerk at 30 *bob* a week.

My time in the Scouts taught me about responsibility in keeping silent about matters raised at troop council meetings and this confidential requirement carried on into my dealing with clients' information when I commenced my own accountancy practice in 1978.

Scouting became an important part of my teens and the Baden Powell principles became my life standard. The induction as a member took place when you learned the three parts of the Promise and the ten Scout laws. Among those laws that I endeavoured to practise there was one that said:

"A Scout is a brother to every other Scout no matter to what country class or creed the other may belong."

Another part of the Law was *"clean in thought word and deed."*

John Moore senior used to organise door-to-door collections for the NSPCC. He got an OBE for services rendered. He had the Scouts out in uniform collecting in the area. He took us across the road to the Short Strand area, which probably had a 60/40 Catholic/Protestant population at that time, and as Albert Bridge church was in Thompson Street in that area, we had no problems. The people there were very generous (I was told later by John).

When what became known as The Troubles commenced in 1969 the Albertbridge Road and the bottom of the Woodstock Road became a flash point. I never got involved in any of the protests but was affected by them because I had become a Deacon in the church. But I still held on to that Scout law, "no matter what class or creed" the people were.

Of course, the Scouts' motto was also *Be Prepared...*

The Scout law for me was soon to become supplementary to that of the Christian faith.

Love of all persons became the new standard for me when on 26th March 1954 I was convicted of my sin, saw I was in need of a Saviour, repented, was accepted by the

Lord Jesus Christ, and with sins forgiven, changed my thoughts, principles and practice for the rest of my life.

My First Job was in the Broadway Damask Company up the Donegal Road. The factory buildings are now part of the Royal Victoria Hospital.

I worked in the factory wages office under Mr Hutchinson and two other clerks. The office of the manager of the factory was next door to the wages office. He apparently thought that I had a little more between my ears when compared with the younger of the other staff and thought I might be capable of keeping his stock record book so that became an additional part of my job.

It was a shock to Mr Scott when I handed in my notice to leave after eight weeks. He expressed his annoyance by using a few expletives that I will not quote and I was satisfied that I had done right in leaving. I believe the factory closed down in 1954.

James Baird & Co

I had applied to James Baird & Co, Incorporated Accountants at that time (Inc. Society amalgamated with the Chartered Accountants in Ireland later) and had an interview, but they gave the position to an older boy with Senior Certificate whereas I, at 15 years, only had Junior Certificate.

Mr Baird wrote to me in November and I had another interview, was offered a position as a trainee Audit Clerk and commenced work on 26th November 1951. I well remember the first pay cheque was for eight shillings and six pence as this was based on £40 per annum as salary. Because I worked on a Monday I had National Insurance deducted for the week. The Salary was based on what was usual at that time - £300 spread over 5 years. £40 to £80 in the last year. I had been receiving £1.10 (one pound, ten shillings) in BDC but my most gracious mother still gave me 10 shillings a week pocket money. I walked to the office every day as it was at 72 High Street in the city centre; walked home for lunch and back again as there was one and a half hours lunch break back then.

I didn't commence my accountancy studies until September the next year as I had started evening classes at Botanic Primary School covering Geography and Ordinary Mathematics with Commercial law. You see, I left RBAI after three years because I thought I would be sitting beside the same boy for another two years, as we sat in alphabetical order. I loved school and learning, so I knew I needed to extend my learning after I left, hence the night schooling from September 1951, of my own volition. During my attendance at Inst. I engaged in playing rugby, cricket, boxing and swimming.

Studies, Marriage (15th Oct. 1958) and Career Moves

I remained with JB & Co until 1959 and during that period I studied at the Belfast Technical College and passed the Entrance Examination to permit me to ultimately qualify as an Incorporated Accountant, but as I've said previously, the amalgamation meant I qualified as a Chartered Accountant in 1961.

During that time I met and married a beautiful girl, Myrtle Anderson, on 15th October 1958. What a great way to start married life – with no savings, for you will appreciate that my low earnings in the first five years did not provide sufficient to save for the future. Although Mr Baird did say "Edward, you know you will be able to command a salary of £1000 per year when you qualify," it was a while before I reached that figure.

I left JB & Co in 1959 and was engaged by Robert Walsh & Sons at an annual salary of £900. (I still had not qualified). Mr William Duffield was the senior partner and I reported to him each morning till I was appointed Tax Manager reporting to Mr John Bacon. Mr Duffield died in the Robinson Cleaver restaurant just across the street from his office.

I have a sneaking suspicion that I might have worked for a short time with Deloitte, Haskins and Sells but it may have only been an interview and I did not take up a lasting position with them.

Erin Finance Ltd

I left when I was approached by a friend about moving out of Accountancy Practice to commercial work with Erin Finance Ltd in Portadown with whom I stayed till December 1992.

I travelled by using the Dublin Enterprise train on the 8.25 to Portadown each day, coming home on the 5.10 train to Belfast. If I missed the train I drove my Lambretta 125 scooter.

Mr Williamson was a lovely employer and the staff were a pleasant bunch – three girls along with Mr Twinem who was the rep. for the Company. When I was leaving, Mr Williamson entertained us at a very nice establishment and then took us all home to watch a Moody Bible Institute Fact and Faith film at his home at Ahorey in Armagh.

He and his wife called at our home in Belfast in April 1963 with a very nice dress for the new baby, Suzanne. During that time I was impressed by the family's evangelistic action in writing articles and sending Gospel tracts to addresses taken from the Irish Telephone book. The Williamson children, Honor, Rosalind, Arthur and Stephen were all involved.

Northern Agency Ltd

Another good friend, also a Chartered Accountant, was leaving the Northern Agency in Belfast and asked if I was interested in returning to Belfast as he was moving to the NPO.

I accepted this as Myrtle was expecting a child around the end of March 1993 and I would be closer to home in case of problems, for we had lost a child as stillborn just into the second year of marriage and there were two subsequent miscarriages.

Children

The first of our two children, Suzanne was born perfect on 7 April 1963. I did reflect that I might sue the gynaecologist as I missed out on Child Income Tax Relief for the whole of the 1962/63 tax year. And on 31 March 1964 when John was born I got tax relief for two children in one year.

Thomas John Anderson McAuley was added to the family. Not quite Irish twins but certainly a big shock and to the annoyance of Myrtle's mum - but to our great pleasure.

We had moved from our first house in 17 Imperial Drive, just off Ravenhill Avenue, to rented accommodation where we stayed until we bought 50 Orangefield Parade in 1961. It had 12 steps up to the front door and a high piece of ground at the rear. You will appreciate that was not the best place to bring up two infant children.

Myrtle

Her mum always controlled what her children should do even though they had other ideas. Bobby had wanted to be a butcher and Myrtle wanted to be a nurse. It ended up with Bobby in the shipyard alongside his dad (his mum said he needed a trade), and Myrtle being sent to Miss Ellis to learn shorthand-and-typing. Having a controlling mother for the rest of her life knocked all self-confidence out of her.

She left home at 21 years of age to live in Canada. from 1953 till 1955 and came back to Belfast really to say goodbye to her mum and check that her younger brother, John, was ok.

In Canada she had become a follower of Jesus and was really a fine disciple. She was later asked to give her testimony at a ladies meeting in Malcolm Lane Mission Hall. My mother shared the leadership there with the daughter of Mr Spence, cofounder of the Mission in 1895.

When I came in from work my mother couldn't stop talking about this beautiful girl. I stopped her praising her and said, "If she is out at church on Sunday I'll see how she looks!" I fell for her at first glance, mine not hers, and we commenced courtship.

I persuaded her not to go back to Canada but to stay until I finished my accountancy qualification so that we could go to Canada together.

She agreed and that was wonderful to me.

Her family lived in various places in East Belfast and when I fell in love with Myrtle they were in 2 Hinde Street. This was the last street off the Albertbridge Road.

Myrtle's first job was in a large linen company owned by the Larmor family who were related to the owner of The Ulster Weaving Company. (The brother, Sir Graham Larmor refused to open letters to *Ulster Weaving* that left out "The" on the envelope.)

I worked for the auditors of The Ulster Weaving Company and I was the staff member in charge of the audit. I remember I once fell out with Mr Larmor when I allowed the junior staff to bring in a radio to listen to the football match between Italy and N. Ireland. The accountant blew the whistle on this covert listening and advised the senior partner. I got a real telling off!

Myrtle held various jobs: including the Co-Op Dairy in Ravenhill Avenue; and the Irish Christian Endeavour Bookroom at Howard Street, where she became manager.

The latter was above the Bible Society office and she made friends with Maureen Burnett who was secretary to the manager Lawson McDonald. As an aside, Maureen married John Dowds and later in life I became professional advisor to the Dowds as well as the best of friends. Maureen is still a great friend but regrettably, though also happily, John is with His Lord.

John and Maureen Dowds

Myrtle moved on to work at the British Egg Marketing Board. She was there at the time we married, on 15 October 1958. That caused a laugh at our reception when my best man said I needed to be careful to count my chickens before they were hatched!

Early Days of Family Life

We bought a terraced house (Myrtle never wanted her name on the deeds of ownership) at 17 Imperial Drive - and I valiantly commenced improving the décor!

Many previous owners were smokers and I well recall the smelly liquid running down my arms as I washed the ceiling in the living room.

17 Imperial Drive

We lost a male child (stillborn) early in our marriage and I buried him in the City graveyard in a communal grave which is unmarked. If he had lived he was going to be called Stephen. Over the next months there were two miscarriages; then in 1963 Suzanne was born and eleven months later, Thomas John Anderson McAuley followed.

My comments were: "Myrtle you wanted five children all boys! So, end of the road, no more pregnancies." She had had several operations which decided the matter, but that was because of her various periods of illness.

When I qualified in 1961 I completed immigration papers as we planned – but the house didn't sell… and soon the children arrived. Then the house did sell quickly and we moved to 28 Roddens Park, overlooking the dual carriageway that runs between Castlereagh Road and Upper Newtownards Road.

Myrtle and I used to walk out after church on a summer Sunday night and stroll past these houses not ever thinking that one day we would live in number 28.

When the kids were ready for High School and Grammar School we moved from there to 4 Crawford Park, just off the Ballygowan Road. Suzanne went to Carolyn Girls and John to Lisnasharragh High School.

As a family we enjoyed many summer holidays together including weeks in Italy, Scotland, Jersey and Guernsey.

N I Electricity

We visited Canada and stayed with my brother Jim and his spouse Hazel. The company I worked for, the Jefferson Smurfit Group, sold the business BB Rentals in June and during the summer we went to Canada for a visit of four weeks before the end of my directorship in September. I had lots of friends trying to get me a job when we were there but none was successful.

I came home and went to work at NIES in the Management Accountancy Development section. The financial director of the Service had been a next-door neighbour at Roddens Park and the Manager I reported to was a former employee of James Baird & Co, Fred Davidson. I didn't stay too long there, as promotion was a case of *deadman's shoes*, or else you had to be a member of the Masonic!

During my employment with BB Rentals I was on the committee of the Radio Retailers Association and made good friends with those who were in that line of business. So I started to do a bit off freelancing as the salary was good, and after I had provided my own car for four years I eventually enjoyed the perk of company cars with all running costs met – a Cortina, and two Audis. I was also given a lovely Triumph 2000 in a hurry at one point after my Audi had somehow acquired a bullet hole(!) and I informed the army.

Accountancy Practice: Self-employed

I had made connections with the advisor to RTRA in England and he rang me when he heard I was moonlighting and asked me to look at one of his clients, as the expenses of travelling from England were too much. I looked at the company. I decided there was at least six months work with some work continuing thereafter on an annual basis. So I commenced my own accountancy practice on 7th January 1978, which I eventually sold on to Goldblatt McGuigan in December 1993. I worked for them as Practice Manager till May 2001 just shortly beyond my 65th birthday.

I had a heart attack on the 7th April 1999 during a church outing on Easter Tuesday which included a dinner at a Coleraine hotel. I didn't make the dinner but was in hospital in Coleraine for a few nights and then the Ulster Hospital at Dundonald.

Myrtle and Her Alzheimer's Disease

We became aware of a loss of memory shortly after moving to live in Comber.

Suzanne and her first husband Colin had gone to live there.

Colin advised me that a bank colleague was selling his house. We looked at it but it wasn't suitable. We discovered that a new-build of 70 houses was taking place and we bought one of the first seven in a location below the other houses. We moved in on 18th December as the first occupants.

Colin (Suzanne's first husband) kept an eye on construction and became friendly with Mr Chambers. I looked at draft plans and asked Colin to chat with Mr Chambers to see if he could extend the accommodation to make the smallest room bigger by another foot, which he did at no extra cost. We were not happy with a galley kitchen which was to make room for an entrance from the garage. This got sorted out, the stairs were removed and the kitchen enlarged. Two other houses of similar construction did not have all of the alterations that we had done.

Living there was fantastic as regards running costs because of the location.

8 Carnesure Gardens, Comber

Myrtle was asked to help Albert Bridge Church with the ladies meeting due to illness of the minister. This meant travelling back and forward to Belfast on a Tuesday. This was supposed to be for one year but it went on for three years, during which time her memory loss increased. Eventually we sold the house and moved back to Belfast to 75 Orby Drive.

75 Orby Drive

I spoke to the Doctor about Myrtle's condition and she sent her for an examination with a consultant who worked from his home address on the Malone Road, He reported back to the Doctor but I did not see the report until Myrtle was nominated for Jury Service. She could not remember things and I had her nomination cancelled.

This report included the word Alzheimer's a new word that we were to become used to in the following years, ten of which revolved around care homes and hospital. The last eight and a half years were spent in Limavady at Cornfield Care Home, where I visited her each day and we were very pleased with the care provided. We were made very welcome during those years. A very good friend, Brian Evans, from church offered to take me to visit Myrtle on a Thursday. This he did till she passed to be with the Lord through death.

Brian and I have continued to meet every Thursday since then.

Alzheimer's - the Worst Disease

When Myrtle and I went to Canada in 2002 she was really at what I call *falling over the edge* stage. It was our intention that we would stay till the closure of the camp at the end of August. We were living in a back room of the main residence on the camp. She was awake most of the night and I got very little sleep. I went to the bathroom with her and she put up with me being there with her. She then wanted to go home and commenced dressing. The camp is well controlled by senior staff but none had any experience of dealing with advanced Alzheimer's. There were around 1000 persons on site, 650 guests, 250 volunteers from different places in the world including probably 50 from Northern Ireland and 45 full-time staff. They could not assist and I decided we go home early.

John organised the changed flights scheduled for a few days later. When Myrtle objected physically to entering the security section, I suggested we have a cup of tea. Sitting the table she suddenly said "Are you going with me?" She went to use the bathroom but turned the wrong way and I retrieved her.

The airline staff were very helpful and used a golf cart to transport us to boarding and our seats towards back of plane. The staff paid particular attention as she walked up and down the plane, watching out that she wouldn't be disturbing anyone. Eventually she came back to her seat for the rest of the six-plus hours. The aircraft was diverted to Dublin because of bad weather over Belfast International. We sat on the plane for another hour.

Permanent Care Home

Suzanne was waiting and we got to the diner near Ballymoney.

Suzanne realised there was a problem and rang the doctor's surgery for an appointment that afternoon. The decision was taken to ask a care home to take Myrtle the next day. Upon a referral by Sheena Kirk, the geriatric consultant, she was moved to Tardree House.

She stayed there for a few months then moved to Ward 4 in Holywell for a short time until they said Myrtle needed a specialist care home to handle her. We took Myrtle to Cornfield Care home and she was there till she passed to be with Her Lord on 5th April 2013.

That trip in 2002 had been her last visit to Canada to see her grandchildren.

* * * * * * *

Myrtle's mother Mary Anne was from a mixed marriage (Catholic-Protestant) and she had married Robert Anderson. Their daughter was christened Mary Myrtle Anderson.

My wife didn't like it when her name was called out as *Mary* in waiting rooms by doctors or other hospital staff.

I didn't put both names on her gravestone.

* * * * * * *

Edward and Myrtle on
their Wedding Day

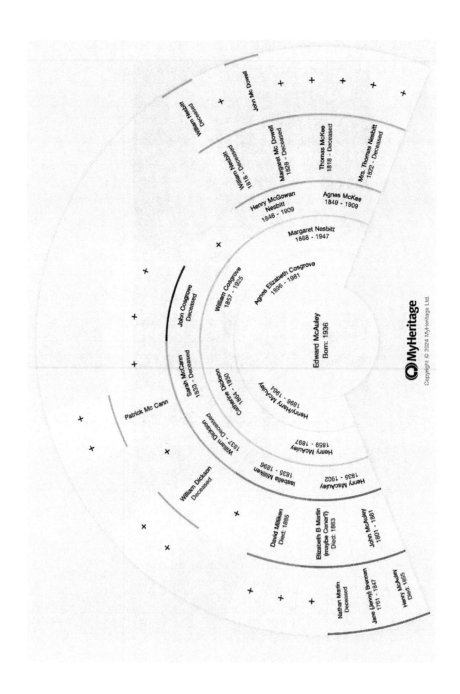

EPILOGUE

Living Well, Finishing Well

As I come to the end of this short collection of "musings and memoirs", I think I probably couldn't do much better than conclude with a poem which beautifully highlights the importance of living – and of finishing – well. It's called *The Dash*, by Linda Ellis.

May God bless you.

Yours warmly,
Eddie

PS I might try to add body to some of the information and events recorded here. Look out – there could be more to come!

The Dash

I read of a man who stood to speak
At the funeral of a friend.
He referred to the dates on the tombstone
From the beginning to the end.

He noted that first came the date of birth
And spoke the following date with tears.
But he said what mattered most of all
Was the dash between those years.

For that dash represents all the time
That they spent alive on earth.
And now only those who loved them
Know what that little line is worth.

For it matters not, how much we own,
The cars... the house... the cash.
What matters is how we live and love
And how we spend our dash.

So, think about this long and hard.
Are there things you'd like to change?
For you never know how much time is left
That can still be rearranged.

* * *

So when your eulogy is being read,
With your life's actions to rehash,
Would you be proud of the things they say
About how you spent YOUR dash?

Excerpts from "The Dash" poem written by Linda Ellis
©Southwestern Family of Companies, used by permission.

Edward McAuley

Acknowledgements

The preparation and publication of this booklet would not have happened without the colossal help of Bill Brodie, his granddaughter Anna (thank you for typing) and my daughter Suzanne.

Printed in Great Britain
by Amazon

45913164R00056